CARIBOU

—A **TUNDRA** JOURNEY—

www.av2books.com

REBECCA HIRSCH
AND MARIA KORAN

AV² provides enriched content that supplements and complements this book. Weigl's AV² books strive to create inspired learning and engage young minds in a total learning experience.

Your AV² Media Enhanced books come alive with...

Audio
Listen to sections of the book read aloud.

Key Words
Study vocabulary, and complete a matching word activity.

Video
Watch informative video clips.

Quizzes
Test your knowledge.

Go to www.av2books.com, and enter this book's unique code.

BOOK CODE

H526284

Embedded Weblinks
Gain additional information for research.

Slide Show
View images and captions, and prepare a presentation.

AV² by Weigl brings you media enhanced books that support active learning.

Try This!
Complete activities and hands-on experiments.

... and much, much more!

Published by AV² by Weigl
350 5th Avenue, 59th Floor
New York, NY 10118
Website: www.av2books.com

Library of Congress Cataloging-in-Publication Data

Names: Hirsch, Rebecca E., and Koran, Maria.
Title: Caribou : a tundra journey / Rebecca Hirsch and Maria Koran.
Description: New York, NY : AV2 by Weigl, [2017] | Series: Nature's great journeys | Includes bibliographical references and index.
Identifiers: LCCN 2016004939 (print) | LCCN 2016008035 (ebook) | ISBN 9781489645135 (hard cover : alk. paper) | ISBN 9781489649904 (soft cover : alk. paper) | ISBN 9781489645142 (Multi-user ebk.)
Subjects: LCSH: Caribou--Migration--Juvenile literature. | Caribou--Juvenile literature. | Animal migration--Juvenile literature.
Classification: LCC QL737.U55 H55 2017 (print) | LCC QL737.U55 (ebook) | DDC 599.65/81568--dc23
LC record available at http://lccn.loc.gov/2016004939

Printed in the United States of America in Brainerd, Minnesota
1 2 3 4 5 6 7 8 9 0 20 19 18 17 16

072016
071416

Project Coordinator: Maria Koran   Art Director: Terry Paulhus

Every reasonable effort has been made to trace ownership and to obtain permission to reprint copyright material. The publishers would be pleased to have any errors or omissions brought to their attention so that they may be corrected in subsequent printings.

Weigl acknowledges Getty Images, iStock, Minden, Alamy, and Shutterstock as its primary image suppliers for this title.

Contents

CARIBOU

Every year something amazing happens in the Arctic. Hundreds of thousands of caribou migrate across the land. In spring, they move north. They climb steep mountains. They push through thick snow. They swim across icy rivers. By June, they arrive at their summer **habitat**. This is where the caribou calves are born. Some caribou travel more than 3,000 miles (4,800 km) on this **seasonal** migration.

The caribou's lifetime journey is their migration. This is when an animal moves from one habitat to another. Migrations happen for many reasons. Some animals move to be in warmer weather where there is more food. There they can reproduce, or have their babies. And these migrations can be short distances, such as from a mountaintop to its valley. Or they can be long distances, like the caribou's Arctic trek.

Caribou are also called reindeer.

MIGRATION MAP

The Porcupine caribou herd migrates to areas in the Arctic National Wildlife Refuge in northern Alaska. Later in the summer, the herd moves to the windy coast of the Beaufort Sea. In fall, the herd travels south to spend winter in the spruce forests south of their calving grounds.

The Porcupine caribou herd's summer and winter ranges are 400 miles (644 km) apart. For other herds the distances can be shorter. The smaller Central Arctic herd has summer and winter ranges that are 120 miles (193 km) apart. The herds do not move in a straight line when migrating between the two places. They travel along different routes depending on the snow and weather conditions. Caribou travel to find food. Their journey takes them over mountains and across rivers, adding many miles to the trip.

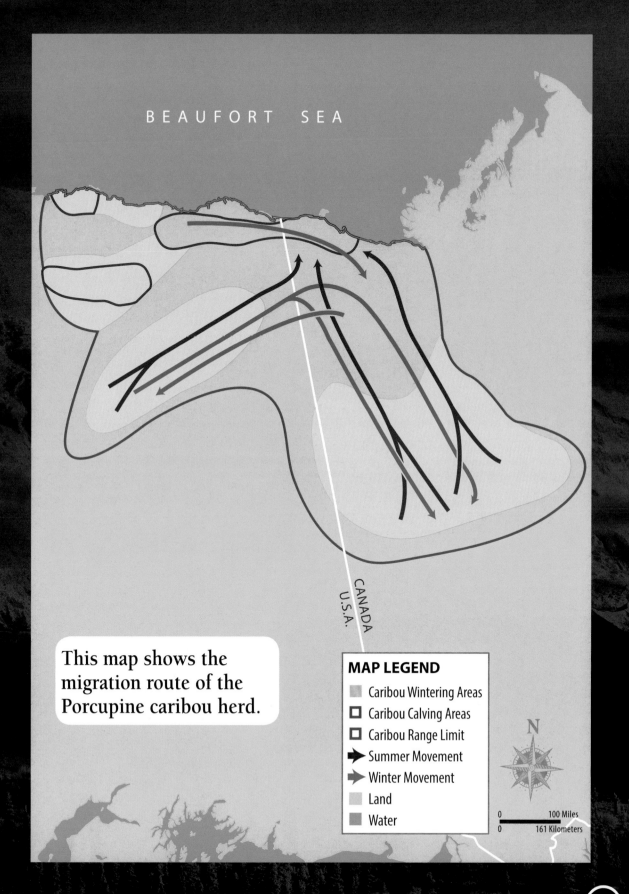

BEAUFORT SEA

CANADA
U.S.A.

This map shows the migration route of the Porcupine caribou herd.

MAP LEGEND

Caribou Wintering Areas
☐ Caribou Calving Areas
☐ Caribou Range Limit
➤ Summer Movement
➤ Winter Movement
Land
Water

N

0	100 Miles
0	161 Kilometers

As caribou walk, they make a clicking sound. It is made with the bones and **tendons** above their hooves. When caribou migrate, the clicking can be very loud!

Caribou travel
in large herds.

HERDS OF CARIBOU

Caribou live in Alaska, Canada, Europe, Asia, and Greenland. They are members of the deer family. They are also called reindeer. Some caribou herds are made of thousands of animals. Other herds are smaller. The Porcupine caribou herd is one of the largest. It has over 100,000 caribou. Although most caribou migrate, some herds stay in the same place all year.

Caribou males are called bulls. The females are called cows. Both bulls and cows grow antlers. Every year they shed their antlers and grow new ones. Their bodies are covered with brown and white fur. Each hair is hollow and filled with air. The hairs keep caribou warm in winter. They make a layer of warm air that acts like a blanket. This layer of air also helps caribou float when they swim.

TO THE CALVING GROUNDS

In winter, spruce forests are filled with caribou. They are the winter home of the herd. Many of the cows are pregnant. Their bellies bulge. They will give birth in just a few months. Wolves and grizzly bears live in the forest, too. They make it a dangerous place for a newborn calf.

In spring, the pregnant cows emerge from the edge of the forest. Together with their older calves, they move north. They are headed for their calving grounds in northern areas. There, with fewer **predators** around, it will be safer to give birth.

At first, wolves follow the herd. They trot along with the caribou, looking for weak animals. But the herd stays together and watches for trouble. If a wolf attacks, running is the caribou's best defense. Caribou can usually outrun their predators.

In spring, caribou move from forests to their calving grounds.

When a caribou senses danger, it rears up on its hind legs. Then it lets off a scent from a **gland** on its hind feet. Other caribou in the area smell the scent. They know there is danger.

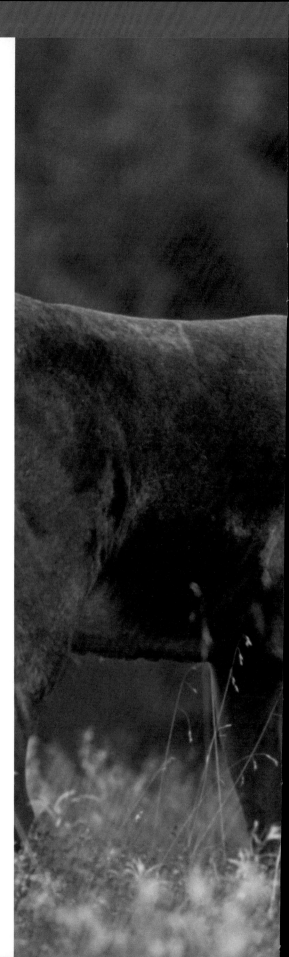

Living in a herd also protects them. With many eyes on the lookout, the herd can be alert to danger while eating. Herd life protects them in another way. When thousands of caribou run, a wolf may get confused. It may follow one animal and then switch and follow another. Gradually the wolf falls behind. The caribou race ahead to safety.

It is a difficult journey to the calving grounds. The caribou climb steep mountains. They walk through thick snow and blizzards. The caribou also cross many rivers. They are excellent swimmers. But they are careful, too. If a river is moving fast, they search for a safe place to cross. Or they wait until the water is calm. In late May, pregnant cows reach the calving grounds.

Caribou antlers can grow to over 3 feet (1 m) long.

In May, caribou reach their calving grounds.

A new calf walks soon after its birth.

NEW CALVES

The calving grounds are on the **tundra**. The tundra is one of the coldest places on Earth. Winters are harsh and long. The ground is frozen. In summer, the top layer of snow melts. Marshes, lakes, and streams cover the tundra. Trees cannot survive here, but other plants grow. Shrubs, mosses, and **lichens** grow well in the short summer.

Pregnant caribou arrive just as the snow melts. The tundra turns into meadows. It is filled with food that cows need. After the long winter, the cows are hungry.

Biologists have observed that male caribou calves wander farther from their mothers than female calves do. As a result, more male calves are killed by predators.

Bulls shed their antlers in early winter. The cows keep theirs until June. This allows the pregnant females to fight for the best spots at the calving grounds.

The mothers need a lot of food to make milk for their calves.

Pregnant caribou give birth in June. Few predators are found at the calving grounds. The wolves that first followed the herd are long gone. The calves are safer at the grounds.

Right after birth the calves are up and moving. At first, a calf struggles to its feet and walks. Soon it can run faster than a person. By the end of the week, it can run even faster. It is faster than wolves and grizzly bears.

Over the next few weeks, the caribou calves and their mothers grow strong bonds. They stay close and play together. Each mother learns her calf's smell. She can find it if the two separate. She calls to her calf. Soon the calf learns her sound. The calf must learn to stay with its mother.

Soon the rest of the herd arrives at the calving grounds. The males and other young caribou join the cows and their calves. All the caribou are thin and hungry. The entire herd fills up on plants.

SUMMER IN THE TUNDRA

Caribou spend the summer eating plants on the tundra. They must gain back the weight they lost over the winter. Cows must gain fat so they can breed and have calves next year.

By summer the calving grounds are thick with insects. Mosquitoes and flies are everywhere. They bite the caribou. The insects are not just pests. Mosquitoes can cause caribou to lose up to half a pint (0.2 L) of blood a day. One fly called the nosebot lays its eggs on the caribou's nose. The **larvae** live in the caribou's nostrils. They make it difficult for the caribou to breathe.

The insects drive the caribou wild. The animals group together by the thousands. They try to shield themselves from bites. Sometimes the caribou shake their heads, stamp their feet, and race wildly to escape the insects. By July the insects are even worse. It makes the caribou move again. This time they go to the coast. There the winds off the ocean help drive insects away.

By the end of August the weather turns cold again. Winter is again on its way. Caribou cannot survive winter on the tundra. The land will be covered in darkness for months. The herd moves south again to avoid the dark and icy winter. They head for the shelter of the forest.

Caribou spend the summer eating.

In the fall, caribou begin moving south.

FALL AND WINTER

In fall, the caribou spend their days moving and eating. On the way, the **rut** happens. This is when cows and bulls choose mates. The big bulls snort and grunt. The tundra fills with the sound of clashing antlers. The bulls fight with each other for the right to choose a mate.

Caribou return to a different part of the forest each winter. That way they do not eat all the food in one place. Caribou are suited for the winter. Their warm fur keeps out the cold. Their large feet act like snowshoes. This helps them walk over snow. Their noses can sniff out food under the snow. They dig through the snow with their antlers and sharp hooves. They find lichens to eat. After feeding among the trees, they move into the open to rest. There they can also watch for predators.

Winter in the forest is long and cold. Even for a caribou, it is a difficult time. Thick snow covers the ground. Caribou have to work hard to find food. The animals grow thinner as winter passes. By winter's end, caribou are ready to move north again.

CARIBOU PEOPLE

Each year, certain groups of people wait for the caribou to migrate. Their migration is important to the groups' survival. The native people of northern Canada and Alaska have depended on the caribou for thousands of years. The people who live in the town of Old Crow still do. Old Crow sits along the banks of the Porcupine River. It is in the northwestern part of Canada. You have to fly in a plane or helicopter to get there. No roads lead to this village. There live the Vuntut Gwitchin. They are the native people of Old Crow. They call themselves "Caribou People." Their town is along the migration route of the Porcupine caribou herd.

The Gwitchin depend on caribou. They use the caribou for food, shelter, and medicine. The caribou is at the center of Gwitchin life. Their relationship with caribou has lasted for 27,000 years. Every fall this native tribe hunts the migrating caribou as they pass near their village. The caribou are fat from the food of summer. The community kills a winter's worth of caribou in just a few weeks of hunting. Everyone in the community helps.

The Gwitchin people use every part of the caribou. They make the hides into warm clothing and blankets. They use the bones for tools. They burn the fat for light and heat. The people understand how the animals live and where they travel. They pass on their knowledge of caribou to their children.

The people of Old Crow are not the only ones who rely on caribou. Many native communities in the far north live with and depend on caribou. For some, caribou is just one animal in a diet that includes other animals and fish. For others, the caribou is the most important animal for their survival.

The Gwitchin people use the hides from caribou to make warm clothes and blankets.

THREATS TO CARIBOU

Today the caribou's home is changing. The Arctic is becoming warmer because of **climate** change. People are adding gases to the air by burning fuel. The gases are trapped in Earth's air. It is making the climate warmer all over. On the tundra, winters are not as cold. Spring comes earlier. And summers are hotter.

More insects grow in warmer weather. The caribou spend less time eating. They may not be able to put on the weight they need to survive the winter. Cows may not put on enough weight to give birth to healthy calves.

Mild winter weather brings thaws and freezing rain. Ice now covers the snow. The caribou have a harder time digging for lichens through the ice. They spend more time digging. They become even thinner. The early spring creates more problems. The pregnant females still arrive at the calving grounds at the same time. The spring plants may be dying when the cows arrive. The caribou may not be able to find the food they and their calves need.

Climate change could affect caribou migration.

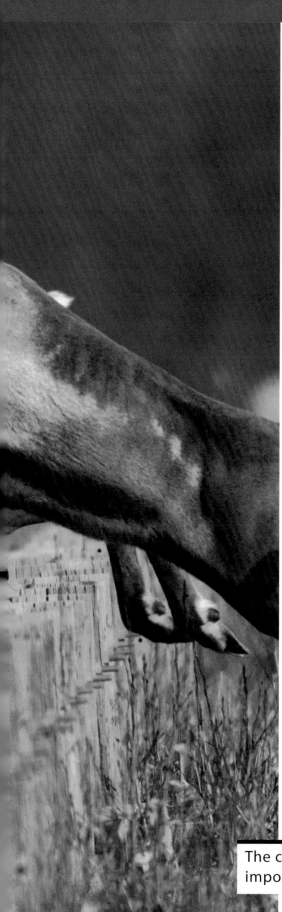

The caribou have lived in the Arctic for thousands of years. They move with the seasons. In a warmer Arctic, caribou may have a hard time getting enough food. Without enough food, fewer calves are born and fewer calves survive.

People are also building in the caribou's habitat. They build roads and dam rivers. And they lay miles and miles of pipelines. Migrating caribou must change their route to avoid these objects. These changes made by people limit the amount of space caribou have to roam.

Oil companies have built oil fields across the North American tundra. Wells, drill pads, and pipelines sit on the oil fields. There are airports, camps for workers, power plants, and refineries. These buildings take up space in the caribou's habitat.

Now oil companies want to drill for oil in the Porcupine caribou herd's calving grounds. Some say that drilling will not affect the caribou. But scientists say that drilling is a bad idea. During calving, the mothers are easily disturbed. In the past, the caribou have left the calving grounds if disturbed.

The caribou's habitat is important to their migration.

Burying oil pipelines underground may be one way to protect caribou migration routes.

Many people fight to stop oil drilling in the caribou calving grounds. They want to protect caribou by saving the places where they live. The calving grounds are important to the survival of the caribou. By saving their habitat, people can help the caribou. Herds can continue to live and migrate across the Arctic tundra.

Caribou often cross the road in Alaska's Denali National Park and Preseve.

QUIZ

1 How far can migrating caribou travel?

A. More than 3,000 miles (4,800 km)

2 When does a new calf begin to walk?

A. Soon after its birth

3 What is another name for caribou?

A. Reindeer

4 When do pregnant cows reach the calving grounds?

A. In late May

5 What do the Gwitchin people use the hides from caribou for?

A. To make warm clothes and blankets

6 When do bulls shed their antlers?

A. In early winter

7 What pests bother caribou in summer?

A. Mosquitoes and flies

8 Who are the caribou people?

A. The Vuntut Gwitchin of Old Crow

9 What makes a caribou's clicking sound when it walks?

A. The bones and tendons above their hooves

10 What is a threat to caribou habitat?

A. Climate change

KEY WORDS

climate: The climate is the usual weather in a place. Climate change affects caribou.

gland: A gland is a part of the body that lets out smells or liquids, such as sweat. Caribou let off a smell from a special gland.

habitat: A habitat is a place that has the food, water, and shelter an animal needs to survive. A caribou's summer habitat is on the tundra.

larvae: Larvae are animals soon after hatching that look very different from their parents. Fly larvae hatch in a caribou's nose.

lichens: Lichens are a flat plant that grows on rocks and trees. Caribou eat lichens.

predators: Predators are animals that hunt and eat other animals. Wolves are predators of caribou.

rut: The rut is the time when animals mate. In fall, the caribou rut happens.

seasonal: Seasonal is something related to the seasons of the year. Caribou have a seasonal migration.

tendons: Tendons are a part of the body that connects the muscle to the bone. Tendons on caribou make a clicking noise.

tundra: A cold area in northern North America, Europe, and Asia where no trees grow and the soil is frozen. Caribou have their calves in the tundra.

INDEX

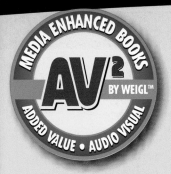

Log on to www.av2books.com

AV² by Weigl brings you media enhanced books that support active learning. Go to www.av2books.com, and enter the special code found on page 2 of this book. You will gain access to enriched and enhanced content that supplements and complements this book. Content includes video, audio, weblinks, quizzes, a slide show, and activities.

AV² Online Navigation

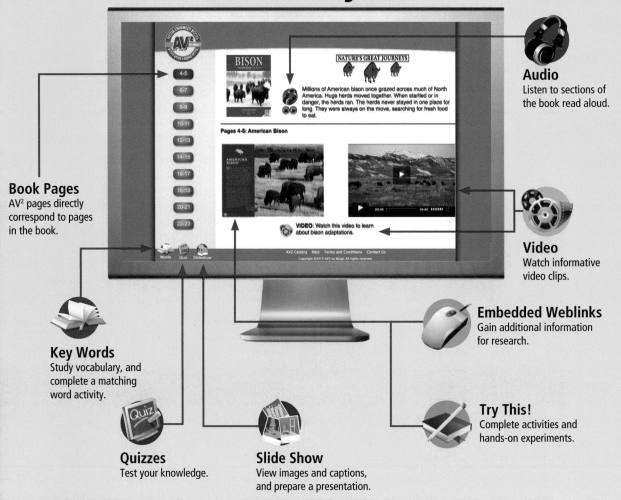

Audio
Listen to sections of the book read aloud.

Book Pages
AV² pages directly correspond to pages in the book.

Video
Watch informative video clips.

Key Words
Study vocabulary, and complete a matching word activity.

Embedded Weblinks
Gain additional information for research.

Quizzes
Test your knowledge.

Slide Show
View images and captions, and prepare a presentation.

Try This!
Complete activities and hands-on experiments.

AV² was built to bridge the gap between print and digital. We encourage you to tell us what you like and what you want to see in the future.

Sign up to be an AV² Ambassador at www.av2books.com/ambassador.

Due to the dynamic nature of the Internet, some of the URLs and activities provided as part of AV² by Weigl may have changed or ceased to exist. AV² by Weigl accepts no responsibility for any such changes. All media enhanced books are regularly monitored to update addresses and sites in a timely manner. Contact AV² by Weigl at 1-866-649-3445 or av2books@weigl.com with any questions, comments, or feedback.